Starting School
Feeling good about primary school by 4 and 5 year old children.

Starting School

Authors Four and five year old children from 4 schools in Kilkenny: Rory Bollard, Niamh Rothwell, Rachel Harnett, Peter Madden, Michael Comerford, Jamie and Danny Fitzpatrick, Thomas Heffernan, Hawna Pedini, Clodagh Comerford, Cionna Vargihese, Dayna Kelleher, William Harford Kelly, Caoimhe Kealy, Jack Cleere Wall, Sarah Heary, Emma Kenny, Emily Kavanagh, Rian Dowling, Katelyn Mc Evoy, Jessica Floyd Ryan, Ben Fahey, Rose Gough, Conor Deegan, Farhan Ayinde, Cian Fogarty, Taylor Healy, Evelyn McEvoy, Conor Tynan, Ali Greany, Jack O'Reilly, Mason Neale, Alan Willoughby, Alannah Bailey, Shayne Stynes, Brandon McCordick, Nathan Roe, Aoife Cafolla, Evie Byrne.

Schools St Canice's NS
Presentation NS
Castlecomer GNS
Wandesforde NS
St John of God GNS

Artist Orla Kenny
Writer Mary Branley
Mary Maher

Partners Kilkenny County Childcare Committee
Kilkenny Education Centre

Published by KIDS' OWN PUBLISHING PARTNERSHIP • Carrigeens, Ballinful, Co. Sligo
T: 00353 71 91 24945 • W: www.kidsown.ie • E: info@kidsown.ie • ISBN: 978-1-902432-95-3 • Kids' Own Publishing Partnership 2015

Introduction

The stages of transitioning into various education sectors has become an area of great interest among educationalists, teachers, childcare practitioners and parents. Thus far, the main focus of transition has concentrated on moving from Primary to Post Primary or from Post Primary to Third level. This publication, *Starting School*, focuses on the transition for a child into primary school. It focuses on areas of anxiety and concern, happiness and laughter, for a child aged 4 or 5 moving into junior infants in a primary setting.

Starting School is a unique book. It is the first of its kind in Ireland to record and publish the stories of children themselves as they settle into their new school setting. We have focused on children in the junior infant years from four schools in Kilkenny, and all of the stories and pictures are based directly on their own experiences, voices and drawings.

This was a collaborative project between Kilkenny Education Centre and Kilkenny County Childcare Committee. Too often in the past, children have moved from one area of education to another without any connection between the various sectors. It has almost been accepted that the sector of childcare was separate to that of the primary school. Children do not finish one phase in their psychological development and begin a new area as soon as they move into the primary school setting. They carry with them their anxieties, their dreams, their socio economic background, their talents, to name but a few. This publication aims to improve the connectivity between the childcare practitioners, the primary school and in particular, the infant teachers. Most especially it will help children understand the world of the primary school and help alleviate any fears they may have, and emphasise the hopes and positives that exist in the primary school setting. It is a story by children for children about an area of transition which is common to all.

I wish to extend our appreciation to Gretta Murphy and all of her staff at Kilkenny County Childcare Committee for their assistance, support and insights provided during this publication. A special word of mention is also due to Orla Kenny and the staff at Kids' Own Publishing Partnership for their creative and practical approach to helping put this project together, and bring about the publication. Finally I wish to thank the Management Committee of Kilkenny Education Centre for their financial and moral support of this initiative, and also the staff at the Education Centre who carried out a lot of work behind the scenes to make this happen. Freisin, bhíomar ag obair le ceithre scoil i gCill Chainnigh ar an togra speisialta seo. Táimid fíorbhuíoch as an tacaíocht a fuaireamar ó na daltaí, na múinteoirí agus ó na Príomhoidí. Míle buíochas do chuile dhuine.

Paul Fields, Director, Kilkenny Education Centre

The transition from preschool to formal school has been recognised as being of major significance for the future educational outcomes of children (Fabian and Dunlop 2007). In Aistear, the early childhood curriculum framework, one of the learning goals under the theme of Well-being is that "children will handle transitions and changes well". Aistear informs both pre-school and primary school and is a significant link which connects both branches of the early childhood education sector. This book acknowledges this and gives voice to young children who have recently been through the process of moving on from pre-school to primary school. Their world has changed, they have adapted to the new situation and here they share their experiences through their own insightful language and drawings.

Starting School is a very special publication because it consists of children's own observations, reflections and advice on this most critical of transitions. It can be used by parents, practitioners and teachers to help children to prepare for and settle into primary school by reflecting on feelings and concerns associated with moving on to school.

This has been a very positive collaborative project between Kilkenny Education Centre and Kilkenny County Childcare Committee. The director of the Education Centre, Paul Fields, facilitated the collaboration between the two agencies most effectively with consistent enthusiasm for the project and his ability with his team to make it happen. I warmly appreciate the creative work of Orla Kenny and the staff at Kids' Own Publishing Partnership in bringing this book from conception to publication. I would like to acknowledge the continued support for this project by the board of management of Kilkenny County Childcare Committee, in particular the chairperson Martha Bolger.

This book would not have been possible without the commitment of the four schools, the teachers and the wonderful contributions and insights of the children and I would like thank the children most particularly. It has been an enjoyable and fruitful project which has supported greater communication between primary schools and pre-schools across the county.

Gretta Murphy, Co-ordinator
Kilkenny County Childcare Committee

MY EXPERIENCES

WHAT DO I LIKE ABOUT BIG SCHOOL?

- Art, colouring and writing, books drawing and reading.
- Learning words and how to sound them.
- Learning to read books and make stuff in art like frogs and flowers.
- On the yard, playing catch.
- We play tractors and trailers and harvesters and we back up and drive around.
- **We have an obstacle course and you have to run, jump, hop and walk.**

-Being happy and having fun.
-Meeting new friends.
-Playing with your friends and no fighting.
-Maths.
-I learned to write.
-We like feeding the chickens (we have a box of newly hatched goslings at the foyer of the school).
-We like switching tables to let everyone have a go at different things.
-You get to go to the library.

We play the violin too.

-We love art. You can paint, you can stick paper down.
-We learned colouring and drawing and reading.
-Reading is kinda hard. You need to sound out the letters.
-I learned how to count to 109.
-I like wearing the tracksuits for P.E.
-I like the uniform too.
-We like going to the big hall for P.E.

-We have a new play area with bar slides. You just put your legs and arms on the bars and slide. There's two little bars and you can go fast but sometimes you get stuck to it if you are sweaty.

I m getting very clever.
My reading is going well.
My brain works very well.

I was scared of all the friends that I didn't know.

-You learn how to not be silly. Silly is slapping or shutting your eyes and walking round the school yard. Number one, it's serious and number two, you could seriously hurt yourself.
-You learn how to stand up for yourself and not be silly. You have to be strong.

MY FIRST DAY

HOW DID I FEEL ON MY FIRST DAY?

-Nervous, sad. I was crying and my teacher gave me a dinosaur and I waited for my Mum to come back. Then I liked school and the dinosaur was still in my bag.
-My Daddy brought me in the car.
-Mammy brought me and I was feeling a bit nervous when Mammy went away.
-I knew some Senior Infants. And I knew some of the names of the children in my class.
-My whole family brought me to school, except for my two Grandas.

- I came in really, really early and my Mum and Dad brought me in.
- First friends I met were Taylor and we started playing Barbies.
- Some friends from my play school were here. Granda collected me.
- I felt good about school.
- I kissed my Mum when she was going.
- My first day, my brother was there.
- I was happy at school.
- Making a friend cheered me up.

I kissed my Mum when she was going

-My first day in the yard I was playing with my friend. I was scared, excited, happy, shy and afraid of meeting new friends.
-My teacher showed us the other rooms, like the hall and the staffroom where the teachers eat their lunch.

The teacher put on labels to help us

-Teacher showed me around. I was a bit shy because I didn't know names. The teacher put on labels to help us.
- I liked school, it was fun. You get to play new games for the first time.
-Teacher showed us where to sit.
-You have to learn to be quiet when you are working and when you are reading.

MY ADVICE

- Know everyone's name.
- How do you make friends?
- Ask them. Say, do you want to be my friend?
- Be really kind to them.
- Please can I be friends?
- Can I play with you?
- Good boys don't make bad faces.
- We line up to go outside and wait till the others go first.
- Don't do bad stuff.
- Don't call names or say bad words.

Say do you want to be my friend.

-At the first break you take out your lunch so you won't be starvin'. You play at little break and big break. You eat one thing at little break and leave the rest for big break.
-When the day gets longer you need two lunches.
-Only girls are allowed in the girls' toilet and boys in the boys' toilet.
-You put your bag on the line to keep your place.
-Play nice at the start of school.
-The yard is the place we play but don't run too fast or you'll fall. There are teachers too.
-Play round the yard and run on the grass when it's dry.

WHAT ARE THE RULES?

-No talking in line.
-Slow down.
-No eating and running outside.
-If you fall you tell the teacher.
-No spitting, no biting.
-Don't stick needles into your thumb.
-You have to ask when you go to the toilet.
-And only one person can go to the toilet.

You have to ask when you go to the toilet

-No boxing or spitting or pulling hair. No slapping, no tripping up, no pushing in the line or playing in the line.
-Fingers on the lips.
-When the bell rings you can't run out of your line. Junior Infants have their own line and you don't mix up the classes.
-Be polite and you can't fight.
-If your teacher wants you to look at the board then you have to look.

Junior Infants have their own line and you don't mix up the classes.

Advice/Prompts for parents

The following suggestions, which arise from the children's comments in this book, may be helpful to parents of pre-school children:
- Discuss feelings around starting 'big school', tease out expectations.
- Encourage friendships with their future class mates.
- Talk in a positive way about school and the role of the teacher - teacher is there to help you, to show you around, it is important to listen carefully to what teacher says.
- Talk about the first morning of school - who will accompany your child to school; who will collect her/him when school is over.
- If possible get a list of classroom rules before your child starts school and familiarise your child with them.
- Realise the importance of the 'lunch box'. Show your child what is in it and discuss what is best to eat at 'first break' and what to keep for 'second break'.
- Encourage a daily routine at home. Use the terms lunchtime, story time, playtime, quiet time, etc.
- Try to develop good communication skills in your child. Help her/him to ask clearly for what she/he wants e.g. 'Where is the toilet?', 'Please can someone help me?'

Advice/Prompts for teachers

This book gives teachers a first-hand insight into the thoughts and feelings of incoming infants. The following suggestions, which arise from the children's comments in this book, may be helpful to teachers of infant children:

- Empathise with children on arrival on the first morning of school.
- Explain classroom rules and routines clearly and on a daily basis.
- To help settle in children, allow lots of time for creative play and creative activities.
- Help children form new friendships through games and discussions.
- To build up a sense of security, bring children on a tour of the school environs i.e. playground, hallway, toilets etc.
- Infants love to move. Incorporate movement breaks throughout the day e.g. changing tables, taking care of plants and animals, going to the library, etc.
- Give due consideration to the 'lunch box' and its contents in the early days and explain that some part of the lunch has to be kept for 'second break'.
- Get a snapshot view of the experiences of infant pupils in other schools.
- Consider implementing a similar project in your own school by asking the current junior or senior infant students to write or draw about their experiences of starting school.